X-TREME LATIN

LINGUA LATINA EXTREMA

All the Latin You Need to Know for Survival in the 21st Century

BY HENRY BEARD
HENRICUS BARBATUS SCRIPSIT

Illustrations by James Sherman

GOTHAM
BOOKS

GOTHAM BOOKS
Published by Penguin Group (USA) Inc.
375 Hudson Street, New York, New York 10014, U.S.A.
Penguin Group (Canada), 10 Alcorn Avenue, Toronto, Ontario, Canada M4V 3B2
(a division of Pearson Penguin Canada Inc.); Penguin Books Ltd, 80 Strand, London
WC2R 0RL, England; Penguin Ireland, 25 St Stephen's Green, Dublin 2, Ireland
(a division of Penguin Books Ltd); Penguin Group (Australia), 250 Camberwell Road,
Camberwell, Victoria 3124, Australia (a division of Pearson Australia Group Pty Ltd);
Penguin Books India Pvt Ltd, 11 Community Centre, Panchsheel Park, New Delhi - 110
017, India; Penguin Group (NZ), Cnr Airborne and Rosedale Roads, Albany, Auckland,
New Zealand (a division of Pearson New Zealand Ltd); Penguin Books (South Africa)
(Pty) Ltd, 24 Sturdee Avenue, Rosebank, Johannesburg 2196, South Africa

Penguin Books Ltd, Registered Offices: 80 Strand, London WC2R 0RL, England

Published by Gotham Books, a division of Penguin Group (USA) Inc.
Previously published as a Gotham Books hardcover edition.

First printing, March 2005
10

Gotham Books and the skyscraper logo are trademarks of Penguin Group (USA) Inc.

THE LIBRARY OF CONGRESS HAS CATALOGED THE GOTHAM
BOOKS HARDCOVER EDITION AS FOLLOWS:
  Beard, Henry.
      X-treme Latin / Henry Beard (Henricus Barbatus).
        p.   cm.
      ISBN 1-592-40014-0 (alk. paper)   1-592-40104-x (pbk.)
      1. Latin language—Conversation and phrase books—English.
    2. Latin language—Humor.   3. Invective—Humor.   I. Title: Xtreme Latin.
    II. Title: Extreme Latin.   III. Title.
    PA2107.B44   2004
    478.3'421—dc22   2003055379

Printed in the United States of America
Set in Dante MT and Trajan   Designed by Sabrina Bowers

Contents
INDEX CAPITUM

◎⧼⧼⧼⧼⧼⧼⧼⧼⧼⧼⧼⧼⧼⧼⧼⧼⧼⧼⧼⧼⧼⧼◎

I. BEGINNING LATIN

II. INTERMEDIATE LATIN

III. ADVANCED LATIN

Author's Note

Although I did the original Latin composition for the first draft of this book, my translations have been extensively corrected, meticulously polished, and felicitously rephrased by J. Mark Sugars, Ph.D., without whose assistance I would have been in *merda profundissima* (very deep doo-doo). Thus, to the extent that the classical constructions herein are historically appropriate, grammatically accurate, and culturally apt, it is he who deserves the imposing, but tasteful, triumphal arch on the sunny side of the Forum, just below the Palatine Hill. If, however, there are any *errata ignominiosa* (boners), it is I and I alone who should be exiled to the remote, windswept tip of some godforsaken island inhabited by rude barbarians. (The Hamptons will do nicely.)

That said, I have to confess that even the most dedicated Latin purist inevitably succumbs to the temptation to make a cheap joke at the expense of the noble tongue of Rome's golden age, and I am no exception. Therefore, in the interests of scholarly integrity, I am compelled to concede that there is no Latin verb *"geronimo, geronimare"* meaning "to express an intention to act boldly or rashly," say, just prior to jumping off a bridge, and if a Roman diner wished to remark, "I will recommend this restaurant," *"zago, zagas, zagat*" is not the way he would have phrased it. The rest of the Augustan yadda-yadda ("*iaddo, iaddere, iaddedi, iaddi-tum*") is as kosher as we could make it.

Oh, all right. Yadda-yadda is actually *blatero, blaterare*. Sheesh.

Preface

PRAEFATIO

pry-FAH-tih-oh

It's often said that Latin is a dead language
Lingua Latina saepe dicitur mortua esse
LEEN-gwah lah-TEE-nah SIGH-pay DEE-kih-tuhr MOHR-too-ah EHS-seh

Baloney!
Nugas!
NOO-gahss!

It's just been taking a long nap
Modum iam pridem meridiatur
MOH-duhm yahm PREE-dehm meh-ree-dih-AH-tuhr

And it's been talking a lot in its sleep
Iam diu autem multa verba facit dormiens
Yahm DIH-ooh OW-tehm MOOL-tah WEHR-bah FAH-kiht DOHR-mih-ehns

In fact, you can't get it to shut up
Re vera, non potes eam in silentium redigere
Ray WAY-rah nohn POH-tess EH-ahm ihn sih-LAYN-tih-uhm reh-DIHG-eh-reh

Look around—Latin is all over the place, like a cheap toga

Circumspice—Lingua Latina se pandit ubique tanquam toga vilis

KEER-kuhm-spih-keh—LEEN-gwah lah-TEE-nah say PAHN-diht ooh-BEE-kweh TAHN-kwaum TOH-gah WIH-liss

Lawyers use it to screw you

Iurisperiti ea utuntur ut te defraudent

Yoo-riss-peh-REE-tee EH-ah uh-TOON-tuhr uht tay deh-FROW-dehnt

Doctors use it to scare you shitless

Medici hac lingua utuntur ut alvum evacues ex metu

MEH-dih-kee hock LEEN-gwah uh-TOON-tuhr uht AHL-wuhm ay-WAH-koo-ays eks MEH-tooh

Politicians use it to hide their tracks while they rob you blind

Magistratus ea utuntur ad operienda vestigia cum te despoliant

Mah-gihs-TRAH-toohs EH-ah uh-TOON-tuhr ahd oh-pehr-ih-AYN-dah wehs-TEE-gih-ah kuhm tay deh-SPOH-lih-ahnt

Priests use it to weasel their way out when they get caught playing hide-the-sausage with the altar boys

Sacerdotes in stupro cum acolytis deprehensi ea utuntur ut se criminibus absolvant

Sah-kehr-DOH-tays ihn STOOP-roh kuhm ah-koh-LEE-teese day-preh-HAYN-see EH-ah uh-TOON-tuhr uht say krih-MIHN-ih-buhss ahb-SOHL-wahnt

Even garden supply stores use it to get you to buy
    overpriced, short-lived houseplants

**Etiam venditores rerum hortensium ea utuntur ad
    persuadendum tibi ut emas maximo pretio plantas
    vitae brevis**

*EH-tih-ahm wehn-dih-TOHR-ace RAY-ruhm hohr-TAYN-sih-
    uhm EH-ah uh-TOON-tuhr ahd pehr-swah-DAYN-duhm
    TIH-bee uht EH-mahs MAHK-sih-moh PREH-tih-oh PLAHN-
    tahs WEE-tye BREH-wihss*

The fact is, for too long these dirtbags have had a
    monopoly on this mighty tongue

**Diutius quidem haec propudia monopolio huius
    magnifici sermonis fruuntur**

*Dih-OO-tih-uhs KWIH-dehm hike proh-POOH-dih-ah moh-noh-
    POH-lih-oh HOO-eeh-uhss mahg-NIH-fih-kee sehr-MOH-
    nihss frooh-OON-tuhr*

But now, thanks to this little book, you too can tap the
    awsome power of Latin to dismay the ignorant
    multitudes

**Nunc vero, huius libelli gratia, tu quoque potentia
    reverenda linguae Latinae uti potes ad indoctum
    vulgus consternandum**

*Nuhnk WAY-roh, HOO-eeh-uhss lih-BEHL-lee GRAH-tih-ah, too
    KWOH-kweh poh-TAYN-tih-ah reh-weh-RAYN-dah LEEN-
    gwigh LAH-tih-nigh OO-tee POH-tehss ahd ihn-DOHK-tuhm
    WUHL-guhs kohn-stehr-NAHN-duhm*

And best of all, you'll be able to insult and abuse one and
all in perfect safety, using a language that everyone
respects but practically no one understands

**Atque haec est optima ratio omnium: maledicere
cunctis hominibus et contumeliam imponere satis
impune poteris verbis augustis quae cum omnes
magno aestimant, tum nemo ferme intellegit**

*AHT-kweh hike ehst OHP-tih-mah RAH-tih-oh OHM-nih-uhm:
mah-leh-DEEK-eh-reh KOONK-tees hoh-MIHN-ih-buhss eht
kohn-tuh-MAY-lih-ahm ihm-POH-neh-reh SAH-tihss ihm-
POO-neh poh-TEH-rihss WAYR-beese ow-GOOS-teese kwy
kuhm OHM-nays MAHG-noh EYE-stih-mahnt tuhm NEH-
mo FAYR-meh ihn-TEHL-leh-giht*

And as you pepper your speech with catapult-powered put-
downs, remember the immortal words of Maximus as
he signaled the attack in Pannonia

**Itaque cum spargis orationem tuam praepotentibus
opprobriis, memento verborum immortalium quae
Maximus fecit signum dans in Pannonia:**

*Ih-TAH-kweh kuhm SPAHR-ghiss oh-rah-tih-OH-nehm TOO-
ahm prigh-poh-TAYN-tih-buhss ohp-PROH-brih-eehs, meh-
MEHN-toh wayr-BOH-ruhm ihm-mohr-TAH-lih-uhm kwigh
MAHK-sih-muhss FAY-kiht SIHG-nuhm dahns ihn Pahn-
NOH-nih-ah:*

Unleash hell!
Solve lora infernis!
SOHL-weh LOH-rah ihn-FEHR-nihss!

And have a nice day!
Et futue te ipsum!
Eht FUH-too-eh tay IHP-suhm

Latin Terms in Modern English

LEGAL LATIN

Latin word or phrase	*English meaning*
in flagrante delicto	
habeas corpus	
prima facie	you're in big trouble
nolo contendere	
res ipsa loquitur	

MEDICAL LATIN

Latin word or phrase	*English meaning*
macula	
fistula	
carcinoma	you're dead
angina	
medulla oblongata	

POLITICAL LATIN

Latin word or phrase	English meaning
pro forma	
ex officio	
per diem	the fix is in
sine qua non	
quid pro quo	

ECCLESIASTICAL LATIN

Latin word or phrase	English meaning
ex cathedra	
in pectore	
urbi et orbi	the bishop is not available
in hoc signo vinces	
sic transit gloria mundi	

BOTANICAL LATIN

Latin word or phrase	English meaning
grandiflora	
tomentosa	
pendula	leafless clump of dry brown
rugosa	twigs in one week flat
sempervirens	

Basic Latin Pronunciation Guide

VOWELS

a	if long, as in "bl*a*h"; if short, as in "rub-*a*-dub"
e	if long, as in "ol*é*"; if short as in "f*e*h"
i	if long, as in "'z*i*ne"; if short as in "z*i*t"
o	if long, as in "d'*o*h"; if short as in "n*o*t"
u	if long, as in "d*u*de"; if short as in "wass*u*p"

There is really no simple way to tell if a vowel is long or short, but if the word is short—one syllable—treat the vowel as short. The last syllable of verb endings are almost always short. If *a*, *i*, *o*, or *u*, come at the end of a word, they're long; if *e* comes at the end of a word, it's short. If a vowel is followed by two consonants, it's long. For other situations, pronuntia utrolibet modo! (wing it!)

DIPTHONGS

ae	as in "*Thai*"
au	as in "*ouch*"
ei	as in "*hey*"
eu	as in "*hey, you*"
oe	as in "*goy*"
ui	as in "*ptui*"

CONSONANTS

b, *d*, *f*, *h*, *l*, *m*, *n*, and *p* are the same as in English. So are *k* and *z*, which are rare in Latin anyway. *j*, *w*, and the consonant *y* don't exist in Latin.

c, ch	always "k." That's a KIGH-sahr salad you ordered. You want ANN-koh-veese with that?
g, gn	always "*guh.*" The Romans were fighting the GUHR-mahns, not the JUR-mahns, and when they gave the signal to attack, it was a SIHG-nuhm (trumpet blast) not a SEE-nuhm (large bowl).
i	always "*yuh.*" It's thanks to YOO-lih-uhss (not JOO-lee-yuss) that we celebrate the fourth of July instead of the fourth of Quinctil.
r	you can rrroll your r's even if they'rrre the last let-terrr of a worrrrd.
s	always "sss." The Roman fanss (not fanz) were ani-malss (not animalz).
t, th	always "*teh.*" Teh-hey teh-rew teh-hings at eak ot-teh-her during teh-he nah-tih-oh-nahl (not nashu-nal) ant-hem (not anthum).
v	always "w." The wolcano that waporized Pompeii was Weh-SOO-wee-uhss.

There are no silent letters in Latin—every vowel (unless it's part of a two-syllable dipthong) and every consonant is al-ways pronounced fully, and often separately. Of course, there are also no actual Romans around to give you the stink-eye when you mess up.

I

LINGUA LATINA TIRONIBUS

Beginning Latin

Narratiuncula—
A LITTLE STORY

Puellae filiae agricolarum sunt
The girls are the daughters of the farmers

Puellae pulchrae sunt
The girls are pretty

Puellae nautas in via spectant
The girls see the sailors in the street

Nautae pulchri sunt
The sailors are hunks

Puellae nautas salutant
The girls say hello to the sailors

O malam fortunam! Nautae male mares sunt
Too bad! The sailors are homos

Nautae ad puellas digitos impudicos porrigunt
The sailors give the girls the finger

Puellae nautas appellant
The girls call out to the sailors

"Speramus naviculam misellam vestram ad scopulum adlisam iri summersum"
"We hope your stupid boat hits a rock and sinks"

Puellae in forum descendere destinant et ibi mercimonium furari
The girls decide to go down to the mall and shoplift some stuff

Omnes paucis annis prosedae erunt
In a few years they will all be hookers

Latin Aptitude Test—

PROBATIO LATINITATIS

(answers below—*responsa recta in ima pagina*)

I. MATH—SCIENTIA MATHEMATICA

All Gaul is divided into _____ parts
Gallia est omnis divisa in partes _____

A. many
   multas

B. good
   bonas

C. small
   parvas

D. warlike
   bellicosas

E. Capture a Gaul and torture him until he tells you
   Torque Gallum captum donec tibi respondeat

II. VERBAL—SCIENTIA VERBORUM

Arms and the man I sing, who first from the shores of
_____ . . .

Arma virumque cano _____ qui primus ab oris . . .

A. Syracuse
   Syracusarum

B. Ithaca
   Ithacae

C. Albany
   Albani

D. Buffalo
   Bufali

E. Sacrifice a bullock to Jupiter so the test gets canceled
   because the teacher was struck by lightning
   Immola Iovi iuvencum ut magistro tacto de caelo probatio
   relinquatur

III. EXTRA CREDIT—QUAESTIO ADDITA PRAEMII GRATIA

Whatever it is, I fear the Greeks even when bearing _____
Quidquid id est, timeo Danaos et _____ ferentes

A. shish kebabs
   carunculas veribus fixas

B. stuffed grape leaves
   folia vitis oryza farta

C. baklava
   crustula laminosa

D. the check
   syngrapham

E. Send a slave over later with the answer, and if he gets it
   wrong, lop off his ears
   Mitte brevi postea servum qui responsum referat atque si erret
   praecide aures ei

I., E; II, E; III, E.

Romulus and Remus Jokes—

ROMULI REMIQUE IOCULARIA

ROMULUS: Why did the sacred chicken cross the Appian Way?

ROMULUS: Quem ob rem pullus sacer viam Appiam transivit?

REMUS: I do not know. Let us cut it open and see if the entrails provide an explanation for this inauspicious behavior!

REMUS: Nescio. Eum evisceremus ut, extane ostensura sint illius infausti facti causam, comperiamus!

ROMULUS: Why do Roman firemen wear red suspenders?

ROMULUS: Cur gerunt siphonarii Romani retinacula rubra?

REMUS: I do not know—let us set the city ablaze and see if their pants fall down!

REMUS: Nescio. Urbem incendamus ut, sintne delapsurae bracae eorum, comperiamus!

ROMULUS: Why did the Helvetian moron throw the water clock out the window?

ROMULUS: Quare iecit caudex Helvetius clepsydram de fenestra?

*Why did the sacred chicken cross the Appian way?

**I do not know. Let us cut it open and see if the entrails provide an explanation for this inauspicious behavior!

***I growl

REMUS: I do not know, but I feel certain that after ten years chained to an oar as a galley slave he will be eager to reveal the reason for his rash act!

REMUS: Nescio; pro certo tamen habeo istum, decem annos vinctum in servitio ad remum intra navem longam, cupidum futurum revelare rationem sui temerarii facti!

The Legion of Superheroes—
LEGIO HEROUM MAXIMORUM

Faster than a speeding chariot . . .
Celerior quam currus festinans . . .

More powerful than a Carthaginian war-elephant . . .
Valentior quam elephas bellicus Punicus . . .

Able to conjugate irregular verbs without making a single
mistake . . .
Potis anomala verba sine lapsu declinare . . .

It's Ro-Man!
Romanus est!

T-shirt Slogans—
TITULI TUNICALES

CARPE NAREM
Pick your nose

CAPE SOMNUM
Catch some "z's"

CAPIAMUS CEREVISIAM
Let's grab a beer

CAVE LABOREM
Beware of work

**MORANS FAC PAUSAM UT SEDES BIROTARUM
   OLFACIAS**
Take time to stop and smell the bicycle seats

PUTEO ERGO SUM
I stink, therefore I am

VENI, VIDI, VOMUI
I came, I saw, I blew lunch

SOLVE LORA INFERNIS
Unleash hell

OSTENDE MIHI PECUNIAM
Show me the money

PARENTES MEI DIMIDIUM EUROPAE DESPOLIA
   VERUNT. EGO TAMEN NIL ACCEPI PRAETER
   HANC TUNICULAM MISELLAM
**My parents plundered half of Europe and all I got was
   this stupid T-shirt**

ABES ETIAM A CONSILIO INSULTANDI MIHI NISI
   LATINE LOQUI SCIAS
Don't even think of dissing me unless you speak Latin

ILLUC IVI, ILLUD FECI
Been there, done that

Bumper Stickers—
TITULI CURRULES

I'd rather be pillaging
Malim praedari

I'm dumb and I vote
Hebes sum et suffragia fero

My child can beat the crap out of your wimpy honor
   student
**Filius meus puerum tuum studiosum laureatum mollem
   deverberare potest**

Thank you for not thanking me for not smoking
**Tibi gratias ago quod mihi gratias non agis quod
   fumum non comedo**

Visualize world conquest
Habe ante oculos devictionem mundi

Keep honking—I'm reloading
Perge cornu canere—sclopetum repleo

Horn broken—watch for finger
Buccina fracta—exspecta signum digiti impudici

Barbarian on board
Barbarus in curru

Proud of our brutal police
Vigilibus nostris crudelibus gloriantes

Stop the aqueduct, save the unicorns
Sistite constructionem aquaeductus ut conservetis
  unicornes

I brake for lunch
Frenos inhibere soleo pransurus

Don't blame me—I voted for Miss Piggy
Nolite me culpare—Suffragatus sum Erae Porcellae

Jesus loves you—everyone else thinks you're an asshole
Te amat Iesus—ceteri te putant irrumatorem

If you can read this, I lost my trailer
Si hoc potes legere, traheam meam amisi

Reality TV—

SPECTACULA TELEVISORIA
VERI SIMILIA

◊⧿⧿⧿⧿⧿⧿⧿⧿⧿⧿⧿⧿⧿⧿⧿⧿⧿⧿⧿⧿⧿⧿◊

Celebrity Shark Attack
Impetus Pistricum in Insignes

Supermodel Food Fight
Pulcherrimae Inter Se Luctantes Edulibus

Beach Babe Lapdance Showdown
**Certamen Ultimum Saltandi Nympharum Litoralium in
    Genibus Virorum**

Blow Job Island
Insula Fellatoria

Nationwide Red Alert Hot Bod Strip Search
**Inquisitio Summa Cum Vigilantia Per Omnes Nationis
    Partes Diffusa Corporum Formosiorum Nudatorum**

Meet the Organ Donors
Salvete, O Daturi Membra Post Mortem

Baby-sitters from Hell Bring Home Animals that Kill for
Fun
**Nutriculae Infernales in Domos Adducunt Feras Quae
ad Delicias Interficiunt**

Big Fat Slobs Eat Shit for Cash
Helluones Squalidi Merdam Pro Nummis Comedunt

Who Wants to Marry a Rich Old Fart with a Terminal
Disease?
Quis Vult Nubere Peditori Capulari Diviti?

Hardball Talk Shows—

DISCEPTATIONES TUMULTUOSAE

That's a load of bull, and you know it!
Merae fabulae sunt, et eas esse tales scis!

You wouldn't know a fact if one hit you on the head!
Rem veram non cognoscas etiamsi frontem tibi feriat!

You're a liberal stooge!
Pedisequus parasiticus es popularium!

You're a right-wing moron!
Stipator stultus es optimatum!

See you next week!
Vos revisemus post septimanam!

Ultimate Sports—
LUDI EXTRAORDINARII

Bass-fishing—*Piscatus Percarum*

Let me guess—you have to drink the beer to make room
   in the ice chest for all the fish you catch
**Ut coniecturam faciam—necesse est tibi bibere
   cerevisiam ut locum in cista glaciei des piscibus captis**

It's a keeper!
Licet mihi hunc retinere!

Stock car racing—*Certamen Curruum Generalium*

When are they going to start running into each other and
   blowing up?
**Quando inter se collidentes incipient in flammas
   dirumpi?**

Pit stop!
Statio restaurativa!

Wrestling—*Luctatus*

Something tells me that the mean-looking bearded guy
dressed up like the Ayatollah is no match for the wily
Captain America

**Suspicor illum truculentum barbatum ritu archierei
Persici vestitum non esse comparem Centurioni
Americano vafro**

Smashmouth! Smackdown!
Ictus in os! Prostratio!

Bungee jumping—*Saltus de Ponte*

How dumb would you have to be to jump off a bridge
with a rope tied to your foot?

**Quam vecors sit is qui de ponte saliat pedibus funiculo
ligatis?**

Geronimo!
Geronimo, geronimare!

Snowboarding—*Super Nivem Labi*

Hey dude, let's head to the halfpipe, catch some major air,
and stick some tricks!

**Heus, laute, contendamus ad canalem nivalem ut aerem
oppido capientes nonnullas technas exsequamur!**

Super rad! I'm stoked!
Maxime radicitus! Flagro!

The Olympics—*Olympia*

I'll vote for the Greek in the wrestling if you vote for the
   Roman in the chariot race
**Graeco palmam dabo in certamine luctandi si Romano
   palmam dabis in certamine quadrigarum**

Deal!
Fiat haec pactio!

Trash Talk in the Colosseum—

CONTUMELIA IN AMPHITHEATRO FLAVIO

You want a part of me? Bring it on!
Visne partem mei capere? Comminus agamus!

Are you dissing me?
Insultasne tu mihi?

You're yesterday's news
In actis diurnis iamdudum es celebratus

You're toast
Mox corvos pasces

You don't know your ass from a catacomb
Non possis distinguere tuum podicem a Puticulis

Your mother is so fat, when she's in town, Rome has eight
   hills
**Mater tua tam obesa est ut cum Romae est, urbs habet
   octo colles**

* Your mother is so fat, when
she's in town Rome has
eight hills

** Kiss my basilisk!

Your mother is so ugly, when the gods turned her into a
  pig, she thought her prayers had been answered
**Mater tua tam turpis est ut cum di eam mutaverint in
  porcam, suas preces putaverit eos audivisse**

Your mother is so stupid, when she found a coin with
  Caesar's name on it, she tired to return it to him
**Mater tua tam stulta est ut cum invenerit nummum
  ferentem nomen Caesaris, huic eum restituere
  conata sit**

Go ahead, punk—make my day
Age, catamite—fac mihi hunc diem felicissimum

Spring Break—
FERIAE VERNALES

Road trip!
Iter faciamus!

Let's party hearty!
Pergraecemur!

Wet T-shirt contest!
Certamen inter mammosas tunicis madefactis vestitas!

Go ahead, card me. See, I've got a Latin ID. I'm 2,000 years old.
Age, scrutare chartam identitatis meam. Ecce, est mihi syngraphus Latinus. Duo milia annorum sum natus.

I'm wasted!
Crapulentus sum!

I'm going to hurl!
Vomiturus sum!

Country Music Favorites—

MUSICA RUSTICA FAVORABILISSIMA

◦᠍᠍ᓕᓕᓕᓕᓕᓕᓕᓕᓕᓕᓕᓕᓕᓕᓕᓕᓕᓕᓕᓕᓕᓕᓕᓕ᠍◦

Si Telephonium Non Tintinnat, Ego Voco
If Your Phone Doesn't Ring, It's Me

Causam Tibi Dabo Bibendi
I'll Give You Something to Drink About

Quomodo Una Nocte Facta Tam Turpis Es?
How Did You Get So Ugly Overnight?

Si Dies Hodiernus Esset Piscis, Reicerem
If Today Was a Fish I'd Throw it Back

Mater Cape Malleum, Musca Sedet in Capite Patris
Mother Get the Hammer, There's a Fly on Papa's Head

Si Me Deseras, Liceatne Mihi Te Comitari?
If You Leave Me, Can I Come Too?

Quomodo Te Desiderare Potero Si Non Discesseris?
How Can I Miss You If You Won't Go Away?

Per Anulum Illa Trusit Digitum Medicinalem, Ac Ostendit
  Mihi Digitum Medium
She Got the Ring, and I Got the Finger

Tu Causa Es Cur Liberi Nostri Tam Turpiculi Sint
You're the Reason Our Kids Are So Ugly

Sine Te Tam Miser Sum Ut Videaris Etiamnunc Adesse
**I'm So Miserable Without You It's Like Having You
  Here**

Caput Dolet, Pedes Fetent, Iesum Non Amo
My Head Hurts, My Feet Stink, and I Don't Love Jesus

Chilling Out—
SERMO OTIOSORUM

Wassup?
Quagis?

Nothin', watching the game
Nihil ago, ludos specto

True, true
Vero, vero

It's off the hook
Ab unco remotumst

Talk to the hand, the face don't understand
Adloquere manum, facies nescit quid velis

Black togas are cool
Togae atrae lepidae sunt

Want to see my sword collection?
Vin' aspicere collectum gladiorum meum?

I'm thinking of taking a catapult into the school
  cafeteria . . .
Cogito ferre catapultam in cenationem scholae . . .

Graffiti—
INSCRIPTIONES LATRINALES

Make love, not war—hell, get married, do both
**Suscipite amorem, non bellum—eheu, iuncti
matrimonio, suscipite utrumque**

Procrastinate now
Procrastina rem nunc

Flush twice, it's a long way to Texas
Evacua cratera latrinalem bis, Texas procul est

If it has tits, tires, or testicles, it's nothing but trouble
**Mammeatae, rotalia, testiculati, omni modo molesta
sunt**

Gods are dead
Di mortui sunt

Beauty is in the eye of the beer-holder
Cervesia pota, pulchritudo cernitur

Yankee, go home—and take me with you
Americani, redite domum—ducentes me vobiscum

If we aren't supposed to eat animals, why are they made of meat?

Si quidem animalia nobis edenda non sunt, quare constant ex carne?

There are three kinds of people: those who can count, and those who can't

Sunt genera tria hominum: illi qui numerare possunt, et illi qui non possunt

It *is* as bad as you think, and they *are* out to get you

Res tam malae sunt quam putas, et inimici re vera te persequuntur

Why don't psychics ever win the lottery?

In sortitionibus donativis, cur numquam praemia consequuntur sortilegi?

Aunt Em: Hate you, Hate Kansas, Taking the dog—Dorothy

Amita Aemilia: Te Kansiamque odi, Canem mecum abduco—Dorothea

If walking is so good for you, why does my mailman look like Jabba the Hut?

Si quidem pedibus ire tam salubre corpori est, cur similis est noster tabellarius forma illi Iabbae Hutico?

Kill Barney

Interfice Arcturulum, istum mimum personatum portentosum purpureum palaeozoicum

Road Rage—
IRA IN VIA

Where did you learn to drive—fleeing from Huns?
Ubi didicisti gubernare currum? In fuga ab Hunnis?

That's it, numbnuts. Pull out in front of me, then slow
   down when you get to the light.
**Euge, enervate eunuche! Ingredere in orbitam meam
   prae me, tum reprime cursum cum biviali lucernae
   approprinquas.**

Now speed up when I try to pass you, and as I go by, give
   me the finger.
**Nunc, accelera cum conor te praeterire, mihique
   praetereunti ostende digitum impudicum.**

Okay, tailgater—time for a brake check
Em, ichneumon—tempus est sufflamina temptare

Big car, little dick
Currus magnus, mentula minuscula

You know what S.U.V.s and hemorrhoids have in common?
   Every asshole has one.
**Scisne quid commune superlativa urbana vehicula cum
   haemorrhoidis habeant? Est unum ex his utrisque
   malis cuique pathico.**

* That's it, numbnuts! Pull out in front of me, then slow down when you get to the light!

** Where did you learn to drive? Fleeing from Huns?

Lady, if you're going to sit there all day yakking on your
cell phone, why don't you stick a steering wheel on
your living room wall and just stay home?

**Muliercula, si vis ibi sedens garrire totum diem in
Nokiam tuam, quidni rotam adfigens gubernalem ad
murum conclavis domi maneas?**

What are you saving those pretty little turn signals for—
Christmas?

**Quod ad tempus reservas ista lumina pulchella
praemonitoria—ad Saturnalia?**

No, Mr. Busybody, I am not handicapped, but you will be if
you don't move your nosy butt out of that parking
place, pronto

**Minime, ardelio, nullo modo debilis sum, sed fies tu
quidem, si clunes tuas curiosas non removeris
protinam ab illa statione**

Don't boot my car!
Noli caligam in rotam currus mei adfigere!

I am too allowed in the car pool lane! See, I'm not alone. I
suffer from multiple personality disorder.

**Certe mihi licet vehi in orbita seposita curribus repletis.
Ecce, non solus sum. Legio mihi nomen est, quia
multi sumus.**

There are three of us here. I want to drive! No, it's my
turn! No fair, what about me? Me me me!

**Adsunt tres. Volo gubernare! Immo, ordo memet vocat!
Iniquum est! Quid de me? Me me me!**

Does that Breathalyzer have a Latin setting?

**Potestne illa machina pneumatodocimastica ad linguam
Latinam accommodari?**

I have Vatican diplomatic immunity. If you give me a
ticket, you're going to end up cooling your heels in The
Hague in a jail cell full of Yugoslavian war criminals.

**Sedes Romana Sacra mihi diplomaticam immunitatem
tribuit. Si me vocaveris in ius, aetatem tuam deges
Hagae Comitis, conditus in carcerem refertum
Iugoslavorum condemnatorum de bellum contra ius
gentium gerendo.**

Air Rage—
IRA IN AËRE

Do you have nail-clipper-sniffing dogs?
**Habetisne canes quae forficulas unguales olfacere
   possunt?**

I think that guy with a napkin on his noggin has a catapult
   in his shoe
**Credo illum mantelium in capite gerentem occultavisse
   catapultam in caliga**

Hey, pal, is that carry-on luggage or did you just sack
   Carthage?
**Heia, amice, utrum illae sunt sarcinae tuae, an modo
   Carthaginem despoliasti?**

Say, miss, didn't you used to work for Con Air?
**Dic mihi, domnicella, nonne te conducebat aëria classis
   quae condemnatos transportabat?**

You know, even galley slaves were served meals
Nempe cibus dabatur etiam servis navalibus

If there's an accident, I'm going to charge people to use
this exit

**Si de caelo cadere incipiamus, vectores pretium pro usu
huius exitus poscam**

Warning Labels—
SCHEDAE MONITORIAE

Your nose may fall off
Fieri potest ut nasus tuus decidat

You may develop hot-dog fingers
Fieri potest ut digiti tui formam tomaculorum sumant

Your head may explode
Fieri potest ut caput tuum displodatur

Your brain may turn to mush
Fieri potest ut cerebrum tuum liquefiat

You may start babbling in Latin
Fieri potest ut Latine blaterare incipias

II

LINGUA LATINA MEDIA

Intermediate Latin

Caesar's PowerPoint Presentation—

CAESAR TIBI PROPOSITA MAXIMI MOMENTI PRAEFERT

I

Argumentum

Gallia, terra in partes
tres divisa
  *Cisalpina
  *Transalpina
  *Oblitus sum tertiae

Topic

Gaul, a country with
three parts
  *Northern Italy
  *France
  *I forget

II

Consilium

*Visere
*Videre
*Vincere

Plan

*Make a visit
*Have a look-see
*Take it over

III

Sequelae	**Follow-up**
*De bello stultum librum scribam	*Write a stupid book about it
*A nonnullis irrumatoribus occidar in Foro	*Get assassinated in the forum by a bunch of assholes
*Acetaria et mensis accipient a me nomina	*Salad and month get named after me

IV

Conclusio	**Conclusions**
*Faciam ut animus meus scrutetur	*Get head examined
*Quid illa femella Cleopatra?	*What about that Cleopatra dame?

Top 10 Reasons to Live in the Time of the Caesars

DECEM OPTIMAE RATIONUM CUR IN AEVO CAESARUM VIVERE IUCUNDIUS ESSET

X. Calculus won't be invented for another fifteen hundred years
Calculus differentialis non invenietur intra mille quingentos annorum

IX. When you're late on a rainy day, you can always blame the sundial
Si sub Iove pluvioso serius advenias, tu culpare semper potes horologium solare

VIII. If you piss off one god, you've still got 600 left
Si deum irrites unum, sescenti tibi iam supersint

VII. Actors are treated like dirt
Histriones foede tractantur

VI. Athletes who complain about their pay end up in an urn
Athletae qui queruntur de mercedibus mox in urnas funduntur

V. Scumbags who get the death penalty think they got off light

Scelesti mortis damnati se leviores poenas pensuros reuntur

IV. The likeliest place to find some pushy Christian preacher is inside a lion

Veri simillimum est, locum in quo praedicatorem Christianum protervum invenies, ventrem leoninum esse

III. The French are an ignorant bunch of servile peasants living in smelly huts, and the Germans are getting their asses kicked

Gens Gallorum inerudita servilis agrestis est, in tuguriis foetidis habitans, et Germani vapulant

II. A healthy diet consists of waiting to see if the food taster dies before having anything to eat

Diaeta salubris est, antequam aliquid cenes, observare an moriatur praegustator

I. Everyone is always dressed for a toga party

Omnès amiciuntur semper togis quasi convivium agitaturi

That Old-Time Religion—
ILLA RELIGIO PRISCA

Actually, I'm a born-again pagan
**Re vera, cultor denuo renatus deorum Romanorum
antiquorum sum**

I get to worship whomever I like, including SpongeBob
SquarePants
**Licet mihi venerari pro deo quemlibet, etiam
SpongoRobertum QuadratoBracatum**

I always ask myself, What would Julius Caesar do?
Me semper rogo, Quid faceret Iulius Caesar?

No, as far as miracles go, this "J. C." never raised the dead,
but he certainly lowered a lot of the living
**Immo, si de miraculis agitur, ille "I Ce" nullos mortuos
ad vitam revocavit, sed tamen multos vivos ad
mortem sane misit**

We're having a prayer breakfast down at the pistol range
**Ientabimus, precatione facta, in campo
manuballistulario**

I am a firm believer in tough hate
Mihi persuasum est odisse acerbe

* Love thy neighbors, and to show you really mean it, send 50,000 heavily armed soldiers to knock on their door and ask in the nicest possible way if they'd like to join your empire.

Do unto others, but do it first
Fac hominibus aliis, atqui fac prius

Blessed are the poor, because they leave so much more
money for the rest of us
**Beati pauperes, quoniam tanto plus pecuniae nobis
reliquis relinquunt**

Blessed are the meek, because we can cut in front of them
in lines
**Beati mites, quoniam istis in ordine stantibus
anteponere nosmet ipsos possumus**

If someone smites you on the cheek, turn the other cheek
and see what kind of a smiter he is with a bloody stump
**Si quis te percusserit in dexteram maxillam tuam,
praebe illi alteram ut possis cognoscere quam fortiter
percussurus sit bracchio truncato cruento**

Love thy neighbors, and to show you really mean it, send
50,000 heavily armed soldiers to knock on their door
and ask in the nicest possible way if they'd like to join
your empire
**Dilige proximos tuos, utque illis ostendas te re vera
diligere, mitte decem legiones quae ianuas pulsent et
quam dulcissime ab illis quaerant, num velint in
tuum imperium recipi**

The theory of evolution is baloney. Everyone knows the whole universe came out of Saturn's nostrils

Theoria Darwiniana evolutionis specierum absurda est. Constat inter omnes universitatem rerum ab naribus Saturni venisse

Of course I can speak in tongues, but I prefer Latin

Sane loqui variis linguis possum sicut Apostoli die Pentecostes, sed malo Latine loqui

Let's say grace: O gods, thank you for permitting us to gobble this food the way Caesar gobbled up half of Europe. Amen.

Precemur. O di, gratias vobis agimus, quod nos sinitis hunc cibum sic devorare quo modo C. Iulius Caesar dimidiam partem Europae devoravit. Finis.

Mob Banter—

CAVILLATIO SODALIUM

It fell off the back of a truck, capeesh?
De extremo plaustro excidit; comprehendisne mente quod dico?

You got a problem with that, paysan?
Num de hoc dubitas, compagane?

Whatsamatter you?
Quid te sollicitat?

Fuhgeddaboutit
Eice id ex animo

Geddouttahere
Noli mecum nugari

God forbid, a piano should fall on your head
Di prohibeant ne clavicinium in caput tuum delabatur

New Age Discourse—
SERMO NEOMYSTICUS

Meditate on this, pal
Meditare de hoc, amice

Do you know the yoga position where you put your head
between your legs and kiss your ass good-bye?
**Scisne schema gymnosophisticum per quod, capite
inter femora flexo, iubentur basio valere clunes?**

Did a dish of potpourri just catch fire, or did someone
light up a joint?
**Utrum patella florum siccatorum ignem modo
concepit, an aliquis accendit sarcinulam cannabis?**

Man, that shit is potent—I am like totally in the
subjunctive
**Mehercle, illa materia tam valida est ut funditus in
modo subiunctivo sim**

I've got the munchies! Pizza pizza!
Esurio! Libum Neapolitanum!

Hollywood Latin—
SERMO LATINUS ACUIFOLIIS

I love it, I love it, I love it!
Id amo, id amo, id amo!

Make the mother the father, change the cat to a dog, and
lose the kid with cancer
**Muta matrem in patrem, converte felem in canem,
amitte puerum cancerosum**

And replace all the love scenes with car chases and set it in
the Hamptons instead of the Civil War
**Substitue autem persecutiones curriles pro episodiis
eroticis, et conloca dramatis actionem in Hamtunis
in vicem temporis Belli Civilis Americani**

Wait, the girl in the copy room hated it!
Siste, puella in scriptorio xerographico fabulam oderat!

I'm putting it in turnaround
Hoc scriptum in purgatorium committo

Pasadena
Praetermitto

You'll never eat lunch in this town again
Numquam in hoc oppido prandebis iterum

Sushi Bar Chitchat—

SERMO IN TABERNA IAPONICA PULPAMENTORUM INCOCTORUM MARINORUM

No mackerel, no eel, and no slab of cold egg crud
**Mihi nullus scomber, nulla anguilla, nullum frustum
ovorum frictorum frigidorum**

When I snap apart the chopsticks, do I make a wish?
**Estne mos homini findenti virgulas prehensorias
aliquod optatum declarare?**

What's the deal with the little strip of green plastic with
the fringe on top?
**Quapropter in catillum poni solet illa taeniola plastica
viridis fimbrata?**

More tuna, please, and another California roll
**Da mihi plus de thunno, sodes, et alterum volumen
Californicum**

How do you get the little piece of fish to stick to the rice
ball?
**Quo modo cogitur segmentulum piscis globo oryzae
adhaerere?**

Are those knives as sharp as they look?
Suntne illi cultri tam acuti quam esse videntur?

You guys make great cars!
Vos vehicula praestantia fabricamini!

Sorry about those atom bombs!
Me paenitet illorum pyrobolorum atomicorum!

Thank you very much!
Vobis plurimas gratias ago!

Computer Language—
SERMO LATINUS COMPUTATORIUS

Download the goddamn file, you bug-ridden piece of shit
Assume plicam damnatam, o tu moles muscaria muscerdarum

If you freeze one more time, you're going straight to the landfill
Si denuo congeles, confestim ibis in fossam purgamentorum

Yeah? Well I've got an error message for you, fuckhead—you're about to be shut down improperly with a ball-peen hammer
Sicine? Nunc age, tibi nuntium erroris habeo, stuprator—mox improprie sopieris malleolo

Car Talk–
DISCEPTATIO DE CURRIBUS

It's a hunk of junk!
Acervus inutilium est!

That car is so ugly, you'd have to put a pork chop on the
   backseat to get the dog to ride in it
**Iste currus tam turpis est ut necesse tibi sit ponere
   offam porcinam in sede postrema ut persuadeas cani
   ut vehatur eo**

You deserve a dopeslap for buying it!
Eum tam imprudenter comparando meruisti alapam!

If the rattle gets too bad, wear earmuffs
Nimium si strepat, indue operimenta tuis auribus

Of course you think you can repair it—you're a moron!
Scilicet putas te currum reficere posse—stipes es!

Whatever it is, it's going to cost you five hundred bucks, if
   that's what it is
**Quodcumque est, Ioachimicis tibi quingentis constabit,
   siquidem est, quod esse creditur**

Try putting it in neutral and pushing it off a cliff
**Vide quid eventurum sit si, dinexo ingranagio, currum
e scopulo pepuleris**

Keep in mind, people in the rearview mirror are even
stupider than they appear
**Tene memoria, viatores conspectos in speculo
retrospicienti stultiores esse quam videntur**

And remember, don't drive like my brother!
Et memento, noli agere currum ut frater meus!

B.S.–
BUBULUM STERCUS

A coyote whose habitat was destroyed by urban sprawl ate
my homework

**Suo tractu operto suburbio extenso, canis latrans
domicilium meum ingressus praescriptum
domesticum mihi devoravit**

Due to global warming, my homework spontaneously
combusted

**Orbe terrarum nimium calefacto combustione
hydrogonanthracum, pensum meum domesticum sua
sponte flammam concepit**

My homework was seized as evidence by mistake by DEA
agents in a drug bust at the wrong address

**In domum meam perperam incurrentes, vigiles qui
exsequuntur usum medicamentorum illicitorum
nimis studiosi pensum domesticum pro testimonio
iniuste abstulerunt**

My homework was forcibly recycled by eco-terrorists

**Praescriptum meum domesticum per vim in fibras
redactum est a sodalitate quae terrore pro Terra
utitur**

* My homework contracted mad homework disease and had to be destroyed.

** Bullshit!

My homework contracted mad homework disease and had
   to be destroyed

**Necesse erat pensum domesticum meum, quod incidit
   in rabiem pensi, deleri**

Strict zoning codes enacted by the town board make it
   illegal for me to work at home

**Praescriptis severis de aedificiorum usu decretis a
   decurionibus municipalibus, mihi non licet operari
   domi**

Because of a lack of statewide standards, the Supreme
   Court ruled 5–4 that I had to stop doing my homework
   immediately

**Normis civitati universae deficientibus, quinque ex
   iudicibus Tribunalis Supremi decreverunt, quattuor
   negantibus, ut pensum statim deponerem**

Small Talk during a Colonoscopy—
COLLOCUTIO INTER COLONOSCOPIAM

Now I know how a Muppet feels
Nunc novi quid Manipupa sentiat

Any sign of the trapped miners?
Conspicisne metallicos sepultos?

Are you there yet? Are you there yet? Are you there yet?
Advenistine? Advenistine? Advenistine?

Could you provide me with an affidavit stating that my
head is not, in fact, up there?
**Potesne mihi testimonium impertire adfirmans caput
meum reapse non infixum esse podici?**

Medical Confab—

CONFABULATIO CUM MEDICO

I'm afraid I have some bad news, doc
Vereor ne tristem tibi nuntium adferam, medice

I've noticed you have no concept of time—I've been
waiting for over an hour
**Animadverti te nullam notionem temporis habere—
nam plus quam unam horam tibi praestolatus sum**

Your handwriting on prescriptions is totally illegible and
shows signs of dementia
**Chirographum tuum quasi demens in medicamentorum
praescriptis nemo legere potest**

Your manner is oddly distracted
Te geris mirum in modum neglegenter

You have an extremely strange sense of humor
Inusitatissima iocaris

Your fees are insane
Mercedes tuae insanae sunt

I think you have a brain tumor
Puto te tuber in cerebro alere

I'll stop in again in a year and see how you're doing
Reveniam ad annum ut cognoscam de valetudine tua

Hang in there!
Perfer et obdura!

Homeland Security–
SALUS PATRIAE

I'd open these bills, but I'm afraid they may contain anthrax
**Has epistulas debitorum solutionem poscentes
aperirem, sed metuo ne bacilli anthracis insint**

The bad news is, the Martians have landed and, boy, are
they mean; the good news is they hate Arabs and they
piss gasoline
**Tristis nuntio Martios descendisse et, eheu, truculentos
esse, sed laetus nuntio illos odisse Arabes oleumque
octanum meiere**

If you don't give me this putt, the terrorists win
Nisi mihi hunc puteolum concedis, phobistae vincunt

If I can't get a decent table at a top restaurant on short
notice, the terrorists have won
**Nisi mensam opimam in popina optima extemplo
accumbere possum, phobistae vicerunt**

If you won't sleep with me, the terrorists will have won
Nisi mecum concubueris, phobistae vicerint

Get out the duct tape—I'm about to fart!
Effer fasciam adhaesivam—mox pedam!

Useful Phrases for Barbarian Evildoers—

LOCUTIONES UTILES MALEFACTORIBUS BARBARIS

I surrender! Please do not fire your catapult!
Me dedo! Quaeso, noli iacere tela ballista!

There is no anti-Roman sentiment here!
Hic nemo est quin Romam amet!

We love your big chariots, fast food, and violent culture!
Amamus vestras currus immanes, cibum festinanter paratum, et cultum saevum!

We hate our wicked and corrupt leaders!
Odimus duces nostros improbos pravosque!

We welcome you as liberators, not conquerors!
Vos non victores, sed liberatores salutamus!

We never liked that dirty old city—it's so much nicer as rubble!
Istam urbem squalidam senescentem numquam dileximus—confracta, multo magis nobis placet!

We'd much rather be ruled by a distant emperor, even if
    he's a nitwit!
**Multo malimus ab imperatore remoto regi, etiamsi
    frutex sit!**

If you see anything you like, don't hesitate to take it!
Si quid videtis quo delectamini, agite, capite sine mora!

We'll be sure to let you know if any Huns come this way!
**Curabimus ut sciatis num ulli Hunni appropinquent
    hac via!**

Have a really nice epoch!
Sit vobis aetas felicissima!

Game Boy Chatter—

HORTAMINA PUERORUM LUDENTIUM ENCHIRIDIIS LUSORIIS

Taste laser death, alien insect scum!
**Oppetite mortem lumine amplificato stimulata
emissione radiorum, cimices extraterrestriales foedi!**

Eat hot lead, Nazi zombie robot commandos!
**Vescimini glandibus plumbi candentis, velites
nationalisticosocialistici cadaverosi automatarii!**

Feel the keen edge of the sword of doom, no-good,
stinking, corpse-eating tomb-ghouls!
**Sentite aciem acrem ensis mortiferi, o larvae putidae, o
bustirapi nefandi!**

I am going to program a simulation of the Roman Empire
and rule it unjustly, cruelly, and incompetently!
**Mihi est in animo programmare simulationem imperii
Romani quam iniuste, atrociter, imperite regam!**

Tax the poor!
Impone vectigalia pauperibus!

Bribe the senators!
Corrumpe pecunia senatores!

Rig the elections!
Falle comitia!

Screw minorities!
Defrauda nationes minores in tua civitate!

Pack the courts with obedient dunces!
Stipa basilicas stipitibus obsequentibus!

Arrest protestors on trumped-up charges!
Infer commenta crimina seditiosis apprehensis!

Invade other countries pretty much at random!
Infer forte temere bellum aliis gentibus!

What could possibly go wrong?
Quid nobis infeliciter fieri potest?

Modern Vatican Latin—

SERMO LATINUS HODIERNUS IN VATICANO

On the advice of counsel, I have decided to testify in Latin
Iurisconsultus mihi suasit ut testimonium dicerem Latine

My patron saint, Miranda, appeared to me in a vision and told me to remain silent
Patrona mea, Sancta Miranda, apparens mihi somnio me iussit tacere

Whom are you going to believe, me or some snot-nosed little boy, no matter how cute?
Utri vos convenit credere? Mihi, an nescio cui puero parvulo muculento, quamlibet pulchellus sit?

Look, these legal fees are putting quite a dent in the old collection plate
En, mercedes iurisperitorum discum eleemosynarium vero vacuefaciunt

What if I say one million Our Fathers and a couple
   hundred thousand Hail Marys and we just call it even?
**Si Orationum Dominicarum decies centena milia
   recitabo, Salutationumque Beatae Mariae bis vel ter
   ducena milia, eritne satis?**

The devil made me do it!
Diabolus me coegit peccare!

Learned Latin for Lovers—

SERMO LATINUS DOCTUS AMATORIBUS

I'm only repeating a query that dates back to the
Chaldeans, but may I ask, what is your sign?

**Si modo licet mihi te rogare idem quod antiqui
Chaldaei suas puellas rogare solebant—quo signo
nata es?**

I think it was Pliny the Elder—or was it Pliny the
Younger?—who first pioneered the concept of self-
introduction by way of the purchase of a libation, and it
is really in homage to him that I am moved to offer to
buy you a drink

**Credo Gaium Plinium Secundum Maiorem—aut Gaium
Plinium Caecilium Secundum Minorem—instituisse
ut vir, qui se notiorem puellae facere vellet, ei aliquid
liquoris Lyaei compararet; itaque in
commemorationem illius iuvat potiunculam tibi
praebere**

Cicero phrased it best, and I am merely quoting the master
when I am driven to remark, "Nice tits."

**Hoc Marcus Tullius optime verbis expressit, neque
profero alia quam ipsissima verba optimi omnium
oratorum cum adsevero te venustas habere mammas**

---

* Cicero phrased it best, and I am merely quoting the master when I am driven to remark, "Nice tits."

** It is required of you to go fuck yourself.

Just as Aeneas inquired of Dido in Book Four of the *Aeneid* after stating his desire to install his obelisk in her temple of love, your place or mine?

A te quaeso, sicut in Aeneidos libro quarto Aeneas, elocutus desiderium erigendi suum obeliscum in templo Venereo Didonis, ab ea quaesivit, tuae domi an meae?

In the deathless words of the great philosopher-emperor Marcus Aurelius, of course I will respect you in the morning

Si me decet immortalia verba usurpare Marci Aurelii, imperatoris illustris philosophici, certe apud me in honore eris, cras mane

Classical Kiss-offs—
VALEDICTIONES ANTIQUAE

Kiss my basilisk
Basia basiliscum meum

Bite my zither
Morde citharam meam

Lick my licorice stick
Linge bacillum glycyrrhizae meum

Suck my aqueduct
Suge meum aquaeductum

Tune my lap trumpet
Tempera tubam quam in sinu fero

Lollipop my toga lizard
Liguri lacertam quae sub toga mea vivit

Lip-read my trouser scroll
Lege labris volumen inguinale mihi

III

SERMO LATINUS ERUDITUS

Advanced Latin

Useful Syntax—
SYNTAXIS UTILIS

IMPERATIVE

Futue te ipsum
Go fuck yourself

IMPERFECT SUBJUNCTIVE EXPRESSING
A WISH FOR THE PRESENT

Utinam tete futueres
Would that you would go fuck yourself

FIRST SUPINE EXPRESSING A WISH FOR THE
PRESENT WITH VERBS OF MOTION

I fututum te ipsum
Go in order to fuck yourself

INFINITIVE WITH IMPERSONAL VERB

Te oportet futuere tete
It behooves you to go fuck yourself

PASSIVE PERIPHRASTIC

Tu tibi futuendus (futuendave) es
It is required of you to go fuck yourself

POTENTIAL SUBJUNCTIVE

Velim te futuas
I should like you to fuck yourself

SUBSTANTIVE CLAUSE OF PURPOSE

Te rogo ut futuas te ipsum
I beseech you to fuck yourself

GENITIVE OF PURPOSE

I tete futuendi gratia
Go for the sake of fucking yourself

FUTURE CONDITIONAL, LESS VIVID

Si te futuas, gaudeam
If you should go fuck yourself, I would rejoice

FUTURE CONDITIONAL, MORE VIVID

Si te futueris, gaudebo
If you will have gone and fucked yourself, I will rejoice

PRESENT CONDITIONAL, CONTRARY TO FACT

Si te futueres, gauderem
If you were fucking yourself, I would be rejoicing

PAST CONDITIONAL, CONTRARY TO FACT

Se te futuisses, gavisus (gavisave) essem
If you had fucked yourself, I would have rejoiced

FUTURE PARTICIPLE DENOTING
INTENTION OR LIKELIHOOD

Oete fututure, te saluto
You who are about to go fuck yourself, I salute you

FUTURE IMPERATIVE

Tete futuito
Make it your policy to fuck yourself

ABLATIVE ABSOLUTE

Te fututo, gaudeo
You having been fucked, I rejoice

You Know You May Be a Roman If . . .

SCIAS TE FORTASSE ROMANUM ESSE SI . . .

. . . you often forget what you were going to say before you get to the verb

. . . saepe quid habeas in animo dicere priusquam ad verbum pervenias, obliviscaris

. . . you think only superstitious sissies are afraid of volcanoes

. . . credas molles superstitiosos solos timere montes Volcanios

. . . you can eat and have sex at the same time

. . . simul cenare et futuere possis

. . . you have ever used a chariot in a bar fight

. . . umquam in taberna curru proeliatus sis

. . . you never make major business decisions without first cutting open a sheep

. . . nunquam de negotio magni momenti decernas sine extispicio

. . . your most recent domestic crisis was a slave revolt
**. . . discrimen apud te recentissimum tumultus fuerit
servilis**

. . . you know anyone who married his own mother or
was raised by wolves
**. . . quempiam cognoscas qui matrem suam in
matrimonium duxerit vel sit a lupis alitus**

. . . you have a statue of yourself holding a sword in one
hand and the severed head of a Belgian in the other
**. . . possideas statuam tui, tenentem manu dextra
gladium, manu sinistra caput amputatum Belgae**

. . . you compliment the chef by throwing up
. . . coquum vomendo in mensam conlaudes

. . . you have a personal poisoner on your staff
. . . unus ex officialibus tuis propriis est venenarius

. . . the only vegetarian you ever met had hooves
. . . numquam phytophagis occurreris nisi ungulatis

. . . your idea of a party animal is a goat
. . . animal convivialissimum arbitreris esse caprum

. . . your car has sword blades welded to its wheels
. . . habeas currum falcatum

. . . there are usually about three hundred other people in the tub when you take a bath

. . . plerumque, cum laveris, adsint in calidario tecum alii fere trecenti

. . . you think it would be really cool to be Greek

. . . putes esse lepidissimum Graecari

. . . you stay home all day if you see a woodpecker over your left shoulder or hear an owl

. . . domi maneas totum diem cum post tergum conspicias a sinistra picum, vel audias bubonem

. . . you're never surprised to discover that the guy running the empire is a moron, a pervert, or a lunatic

. . . numquam admireris te invenire gubernatorem imperii fatuum esse, vel pravum, vel vesanum

Restaurant 'Tude—
BILIS IN POPINA

My name is Sir—I'll be your customer tonight
Nomen mihi est Dominus—hodie vobiscum cenabo

My sign is, I sign the check
Natus sum signo signantis syngrapham

The only thing I wish to know about you is where the hell
 you are when I want something
**De te scire volo solum ubi gentium sis cum alicuius
 indigeam**

If those entrées are so special, why aren't they on the
 menu?
**Si quidem illa fercula tantum praestant, cur in
 epularum indice non sunt?**

Exactly how fresh is that pepper?
Quam recenter lectum est hoc piper?

Why do you put it in a mill the size of a war-trumpet?
Quamobrem id ponis in molina tanta quanta tuba est?

This is indeed a very impressive wine list, if you're in the
mood for a bottle of grape-flavored rust remover that
costs as much as a new sofa

**Haec tabula vinorum grandia pollicetur cuicumque sit
in animo bibere ex ampulla liquoris qui sapit uvas et
solvit ferruginem et stat tanti quanti lectus novus**

My compliments to the chef—the empire lost a truly
inspired poisoner when he decided to go to cooking
school

**Summam coquo laudem tribuo—imperium venefico
ingeniosissimo privatum est cum ille scholam
coquinariam obire statuit**

No dessert, thanks, unless it contains the antidote

**Benigne, secundam mensam non requiro, nisi
antidotum continet**

I'd have written in a smaller tip but there is no Roman
numeral for a nickel

**In syngrapha munusculum minus inscripsissem, sed
non est littera Romana quae Ioachimici vicesimam
significat**

I'll be sure to recommend this place to my friends

Zago, zagas, zagat

Winespeak—
DICTA ARBITRI VINI

It's an intense chalky white marked by overtones of
    turpentine and lead, with a bright, long-lasting finish
**Vinum peralbum cretosum est, resinam terebinthinam
et cerussam redolens, nec sine polimine nitido
durabili**

It's a pointless little red wine with a unique balance of
    ignorance and pretension made by an obnoxious
    millionaire Napa Valley dilettante for self-important
    dumb-lucky dickheads just like him
**Vinum irritum pusillum rubrum est, incomparabiliter
librans ignorantiam suam cum ostentatione, a
quodam Trimalchione Napaensi confectum salaputiis
gloriosis immerito fortunatis, persimilibus sui**

It's a dirt-cheap head-banging screw-top bum wine that I
    poured into a leftover bottle with a fancy French label
    while no one was looking
**Vappa vilissima est, quae capitis dolores facit, quamque
ex lagona obturamento versatili clausa in lagunculam
reliquam, cui pittacium Gallicum speciosum affixum
erat, transfudi, dum nemo me spectabat**

Vappa vilissima est, quae capitis dolores facit, quamque ex lagona obturamento versatili clausa in lagunculam reliquam, cui pittacium Gallicum speciosum affixum erat, transfudi dum nemo me spectabat. *

Summam coquo laudem tribuo— imperium venefico ingeniosissimo privatum est cum ille scholam coquinariam obire statuit. **

* It's a dirt-cheap head-banging screw-top bum wine that I poured into a leftover bottle with a fancy French label while no one was looking.

** My compliments to the chef—the empire lost a truly inspired poisoner when he decided to go to cooking school.

The Bestseller List—

TABULA LIBRORUM
VENDIBILISSIMORUM

◎⧼⧽⧼⧽⧼⧽⧼⧽⧼⧽⧼⧽⧼⧽⧼⧽⧼⧽⧼⧽⧼⧽⧼⧽⧼⧽◎

Quick and Easy Decorating Secrets That Let You Turn a Rustic Hovel into a Charming Country Home without Busting Your Budget by Vitruvius

Artis Ornatus Arcana Per Quae Casa Tua Rustica Celeriter Expediteque Converti Potest in Villam Venustam Sine Sumptu Extra Modum Vitruvius Pollio scripsit

Toujours, Gaul by Julius Caesar
Semper, Gallia C. Iulius Caesar scripsit

Eat Right—for that Lean and Hungry Look! by Cassius
Edi Recte—ut Speciem Macram et Ieiunam Geras auctore C. Cassio Longino

Great-Tasting Hot Meals Your Slaves Can Whip Up in Two Days or Less by Cato the Elder
Edulia Calida Sapidissimaque quae Familia Tua Potest Parare Duobus Diebus vel Uno M. Porcius Cato descripsit

Cleopatra's Hour-a-Day Bun-Firming Love-Muscle Sexercise
Workout by Mark Antony
De Cleopatrae Callipygiana Exercitatione Aphrodisiaca
Per Unam Horam in Singulos Dies Musculorum
Venereorum M. Antonius scripsit

Letters to My Cat by Pliny the Younger
Epistulae ad Felem Suam quas C. Plinius Caecilius
Secundus scripsit

What Color is Your Catapult? by Frontinus
Cuius Coloris est Catapulta Tua? Sextus Iulius
Frontinus scripsit

Oracles Say the Darnedest Things by Livy
Oraculis Inusitatissima Enuntiantur
Titus Livius scripsit

Entrail Reading for Dummies by Cicero
Haruspicium Stipitibus Explicat M. Tullius Cicero

Men Are from Troy, Women Are from Greece by Virgil
E Troia Viri, Ex Graecia Feminae Oriuntur P. Virgilius
Maro scripsit

Now You Can Lose Weight without Vomiting with the
Revolutionary Lark's Tongue Diet by Apicius
Nunc Adipem Deponere Potes Sine Vomitu per
Diaetam Novam atque Inauditam Quae Linguarum
Alaudarum Esum Praescribit L. Apicius scripsit

Latin for Trekkies—

SERMO LATINUS
SECTATORIBUS
PEREGRINATIONIS ASTRALIS

Our shields are down to 25 percent and those stupid sparks
are coming out of all the control panels!

**Scutorum nostrorum potestatis remanet solummodo
quarta pars, et istae scintillae ridiculae ex omnibus
claviaturis gubernatoriis evolant!**

We're being controlled by a subordinating conjunction of
time implying purpose or intent

**Coercemur coniunctione subiunctiva temporali quae
propositum vel intentionem significat**

Resistance is futile. Prepare to be assimilated into the
subjunctive.

**Resistere irritum est. Praeparate vos ad translationem
in modum subiunctivum.**

It's our only hope. Activate the transitive verbs and engage
the ablative of separation.

**Hoc sola spes nobis est. Verbis transitivis citis, adhibe
casum ablativum separationis.**

We're entering the future perfect indicative. We'll only have one chance to achieve a case shift.

Intramus tempus futurum perfectum modo indicativo. Unam tantum occasionem habebimus mutandi casum.

We're slipping into the passive. Quick, reroute all available power to the verb endings.

In genus passivum labimur. Inmitte cito impetum omnem quem in promptu habemus in terminationes verborum.

We have entered. We shall have entered! Do be entering!

Intravimus! Intraverimus! Intratote!

To be continued . . .

Narratio resumetur . . .

Attack Ads–

PRAECONIUM PROCAX CANDIDATORUM

Ask my opponent why he wants to put a tax on Bibles and
American flags to buy gourmet meals for convicted
murderers

**Quaerite a competitore meo cur vectigal Bibliis Sacris et
vexillis Americanis imponere velit ad epulas
comparandas homicidis condemnatis**

Call my opponent and demand that he stop accepting
campaign contributions from operators of nursing-
home casinos, publishers of pornographic children's
books, and owners of Mexican puppy mills

**Vocantes competitorem meum poscite ut desinat
accipere ad ambitionem alendam dona vel ab eis qui
virginibus puerisque libros edunt Sotadicos, vel ab
eis qui aleatoria in gerontocomiis apparant, vel ab eis
qui catellos in Hispania Nova immodice alunt**

* Ask my opponent why he wants to put a tax on Bibles and American flags to buy gourmet meals for convicted murderers

** Tell my opponent you oppose his plan to sponsor a law forcing Sunday schools to hire unemployed bilingual homosexual drug addicts

Tell my opponent you oppose his plan to sponsor a law
  forcing Sunday schools to hire unemployed bilingual
  homosexual drug addicts

**Dicite competitori meo vos obstare proposito suo
  ferendi legem quae cogat ludos Dominicales
  conducere paedicatores otiosos bilingues
  narcomaniacos**

Business Latin—
SERMO LATINUS NEGOTIALIS

I respectfully decline to answer on the grounds that
anything I might say would be a bald-faced lie
**Recuso reverenter ne respondeam, quia quicquid dicam
id sit mendacium impudens**

It wasn't all done with smoke and mirrors—there were
some bells and whistles, too
**Non solum fumo speculisque, sed etiam tintinnabulis
fistulisque factum est**

It wasn't really a loss, it was a loan, which of course shows
up as a profit
**Non vero damnum erat sed mutuum, quod scilicet in
rationibus existimatur lucrum**

I was out of the loop, but I distinctly remember asking if it
passed the smell test
**Consilii particeps non eram, tamen memini clare me
rogare num id insidias oleret**

Due to an alien abduction, I have no recollection of
anything else during that particular period of time
**Quod raptus sum a transaetheriis, omnia quae
evenerunt illo tempore de memoria mea exciderunt**

I only sold my stock because a gypsy fortune-teller told me
  it was an unlucky month for any company with a vowel
  in its name
**Omnes partes meas vendidi tantummodo eo, quod
  Aegyptia sortilega mihi dixit mensem infaustum esse
  cuiquam societati quae vocalem in nomine habet**

Plus which, I needed cash to buy a condominium for my
  daughter's hamster
**Mihi autem pecunia opus erat ad domicilium emendum
  criceto filiae meae**

I mistook the shredder for a Xerox machine
Discissorem esse Xerographium perperam putavi

Look, let me off the hook and I will rat out every single
  person in the whole company
**Age, da mihi veniam ac impunitatem, deferam
  unumquemque hominum in societate**

Furat Emptor—

LET THE BUYER GO MAD

Ministerium consultatorium rerum technicarum tibi
gratias agit quod vocavisti
Thank you for calling tech support

Verisimile est te haudquaquam intellegere quod dicimus;
quid enim?
**You probably don't understand a word we're saying;
but so what?**

Vocatum tuum nullius momenti putamus eumque
neglegemus in ordine
**Your call is of no interest to us and will be ignored in
the order it was received**

Fieri potest ut vocatum tuum subauscultemus vel
transcribamus animi causa
**Your call may be monitored or recorded to provide us
with entertainment**

Omnes auxiliatores nostri nunc emptores alios furiant
**All of our representatives are currently driving other
customers crazy**

Necesse tibi est morari circa tres dies et dimidiam
**Your approximate waiting time is three and one-half
days**

Preme bullulam primam uti musicam molestam audias
Press one to hear irritating music

Preme secundam ut sonum funis occupati audias
Press two to hear a busy signal

Preme tertiam uti tinnitum sempiternum lineae vacuae
audias
**Press three for the endless ringing of a non-working
extension**

Preme quartam uti statim disiungaris
Press four to be immediately disconnected

Sit iucundus tibi dies
Have a nice day

Jury Duty—
OFFICIUM IUDICIALE

I'm hopelessly prejudiced—everyone in this court looks
like a criminal, including the judge

**Opinionem praeiudicatam immutabilem habeo—omnes
in hac basilica mihi videri nefarios esse, praetore non
excepto**

No fair! Just last month I served as a hooded judge on a
secret military tribunal, but they made me promise not
to tell.

**Iniquum est! Modo proximo mense officio iudicis
cucullati functus sum in tribunali clandestino militari
tamen coactus sum iurare me de eo taciturum.**

I swear to tell the truth, the whole truth, and nothing but
the truth, so help, help me Rhonda

**Iuro sollemniter me dicturum verum, totum verum,
nihil praeter verum, ita me iuvet, iuvet Rhonda**

I think I can tell if someone is guilty just by looking at
them

**Credo me posse diiudicare utrum quis nocens an
innocens sit modo eum spectando**

* I swear to tell the truth, the whole truth, and nothing but the truth, so help, help me Rhonda

** I think I can tell if someone is guilty just by looking at them

*** If it's really, really close and the jury deadlocks, is it okay to flip a coin?

If it's really, really close and the jury deadlocks, is it okay
to flip a coin?

**Si lis valde dubia sit, sententiis iuratorum paribus,
liceatne nos nummum iactare, "caput aut navem"
enuntiantes?**

If the guy is obviously guilty, can we just skip the trial and
send him straight to prison under early admission?

**Si reus manifesto sit in culpa, sitne fas nos quaestionem
praetereuntes condemnatum in carcerem confestim
conicere per admissionem subitariam?**

If the gloves don't fit, do we have·to acquit?

**Si digitalia non congruant manibus, sitne nobis necesse
reum absolvere?**

Does the jury room have a minibar?

**Estne cubiculum deliberationis instructum cistula
potionum spirituosarum?**

I believe the minimum award in civil cases should be one
million dollars, but if you lose, you get the electric chair

**Mea sententia, causam privatam obtinenti ut minimum
decies centena milia Ioachimicorum addici debent, at
de perdente supplicium ultimum in electrica sella
sumendum est**

I plan to find everyone not guilty by reason of I am
extremely pissed off

**In animo mihi est, iracundiae meae maximae causa,
quemque reum absolvere de crimine**

But in a larger sense, can any of us say that we are truly
   innocent?
**Quod autem ad res universas attinet, ecquis nostrum.
   dicere potest se vere innocentem esse?**

No, no! It was me! It was me all along! I did it! I did it and
   I'm glad! Ha-ha, just kidding.
**Minime! Non est! Ego fui! Semper ego! Ego facinus feci!
   Atque gaudeo me fecisse! Hahahae! Tantummodo
   iocabar.**

Stealth Latin–
SERMO LATINUS CLANDESTINUS

What you say in Latin
What you say it means
What it really means

Stupra fascino volanti torum pistrinum provolventem.
You never cease to amaze me with your deeply insightful remarks.
Go take a flying fuck at a rolling doughnut.

Quin futuis uxorem tuam foedam?
Why doesn't everyone recognize your genius?
Why don't you go screw your ugly wife?

Velim caput tuum devellere deinde in confinium gulae cacare.
I just want to tell you how much I appreciate your constructive criticism.
I'd like to rip off your head and take a dump in the hole.

Mande merdam et morere.
Keep up the good work.
Eat shit and die.

Propudium parcissimum.
I'll get the check.
You cheap bastard.

Carrus exsecrabilis est! Venditor te irrumavit!
What a great car! You got a heck of a deal!
What a piece of shit! You got taken to the cleaners!

Aspice hanc supellectilem vilem. Quale gurgustium est.
Fabulous house—I love your taste.
Look at this cheesy crap. What a dump.

Rotaturne capitulum huius, virus exspuens viride?
Well, now, really, isn't that the cutest baby you've ever
    seen?
Does its head spin around and spit green slime?

**Speciem scurrae habes. Spectaculum petauristarum
    bestiarumque nesciebam adesse.**
Dynamite outfit! It really looks good on you.
You look like a clown. I didn't know the circus was in town.

**Amicus tuus expers rationis est. Viculus nescioquis
    barone suo privatus est.**
Your boyfriend is a great guy. No wonder you've been
    keeping him to yourself.
He's a total moron. Somewhere there's a village missing its idiot.

Amica tua est originis extraterrestrialis. Si fortuna tibi faveat, cum astronavem suam ista refecerit, a terra tuaque vita discedet tam cito quam fulmen ascendit.

Your girlfriend is a knockout. Talent, beauty, brains—she has it all.

She's a space alien. If you're lucky, when she gets her flying saucer fixed, she'll be out of here and out of your life in a flash.

Stealth Latin for Golfers—

SERMO LATINUS CLANDESTINUS IN LUSU CALEDONIO

Quod fustuarium!
Nice swing!
What a hack!

Salaputium fortunatum!
Great shot!
You lucky fuckhead.

Seligatur clava imprudenter
Be the right club.
Be the wrong club.

Pilula, curre in harenariam et defode te.
Hurry up ball, get some air! Be there!
Get in that bunker and bury.

Vola! Aberra! Egredere praeter terminos!
Stop! Hit something! Stay in play!
Go! Get lost, ball! Go out of bounds!

Immerge te in aquam!
Stay dry!
Get wet!

Decurre ab area leni in gramen densum!
Sit down! Bite!
Run off the green into the rough!

Transili puteolum!
Go in the hole!
Lip out!

Euax!
Aww, too bad!
Hurray!

Bad Latin, the Dirty Dozen—

SERMO LATINUS IMPUDICUS: DUODECIM OBSCENA

asshole	*culus, i* m.;
	podex, podicis, m.
balls	*coleus, i* m.;
to be blown	*irrumo, irrumare*
& to blow	*fello, fellare; ligurio, ire;*
	(verpam) comedo, esse, edi, estum
to bugger	*pedico, are*
butt	*clunis, is* m. & f. *(clunes, ium);*
	natis, is f. *(nates, ium);*
	puta, ae f.
cock	*capulus, i* m.; *cauda, ae* f.; *cicer, is* n.; *clavus, i* m.; *cucumis,*
	eris m.; *falcula, ae* f.; *fascinum, i* n.; *gladius, i* m.; *hasta, ae* f.;
	membrum, i n.; *mentula, ae* f.; *peculium, i* n.; *radix, icis* f.;
	rutabulum, i n.; *sicula, ae* f.; *telum, i* n.; *verpa, ae* f.; *vomer, eris* m.
cunt	*aratiuncula, ae* f.;
	cunnus, i m.
fart, to fart	*crepitus, us.* m.:
	strepitus, us m.;

	crepo, crepare, crepui, crepitum; pedo, pedere,
	pepedi, peditum; strepito, are
to fuck	*concumbo, concumbere, concubui, concubitum;*
	futuo, futuere, futui, fututum
to jerk off	*frico, fricare, fricui, frictum (fricatum);*
	percieo, ire, ivi, itum;
	sollicito, are;
	tero, terere, trivi, tritum;
	tracto, tractare
piss, to piss	*urina, ae* f.;
	meio, meiere, mixi, mictum;
	mingo, mingere, minxi, minctum
shit, to shit	*fimus, i* m. *& fimus, i* n.;
	merda, ae f.;
	stercus, oris n.;
	caco, are